COLLEGE GOATs

THE GREATEST OF ALL TIME

GOATs OF COLLEGE WOMEN'S BASKETBALL

BY LUKE HANLON

SportsZone

An Imprint of Abdo Publishing
abdobooks.com

abdobooks.com

Published by Abdo Publishing, a division of ABDO, PO Box 398166, Minneapolis, Minnesota 55439.

Printed in the United States of America, North Mankato, Minnesota.
102025
012026

Cover Photo: G. Fiume/Getty Images Sport/Getty Images
Interior Photos: John G. Zimmerman/Sports Illustrated/Getty Images, 4; Bettmann/Getty Images, 7; Richard Mackson/Sports Illustrated/Getty Images, 8; David Madison/Getty Images Sport/Getty Images, 11; Joe Patronite/Getty Images Sport/Getty Images, 12; Otto Greule Jr./Getty Images Sport/Getty Images, 14–15; Damian Strohmeyer/Allsport/Hulton Archive/Getty Images, 16; Elise Amendola/AP Images, 18–19; Jonathan Daniel/Allsport/Getty Images Sport/Getty Images, 20; Michael Conroy/AP Images, 23; Jay L. Clendenin/NCAA Photos/Getty Images, 24, 28; Elsa/Getty Images Sport/Getty Images, 27; Ronald Martinez/Getty Images Sport/Getty Images, 31, 32; Jamie Schwaberow/NCAA Photos/Getty Images, 35; Andy Lyons/Getty Images Sport/Getty Images, 36, 43; Tony Quinn/Icon Sportswire/Getty Images, 38–39; Matthew Holst/Getty Images Sport/Getty Images, 40

Editor: Dalton Rains
Series Designer: Kate Liestman

Library of Congress Control Number: 2025939142

Publisher's Cataloging-in-Publication Data

Names: Hanlon, Luke, author.
Title: GOATS of college women's basketball / by Luke Hanlon
Description: Minneapolis, Minnesota: Abdo Publishing, 2026 | Series: College GOATs: the greatest of all time | Includes online resources and index.
Identifiers: ISBN 9781098298357 (lib. bdg.) | ISBN 9798384932154 (ebook)
Subjects: LCSH: College sports--Juvenile literature. | Basketball--Juvenile literature. | Women college athletes--Juvenile literature. | College sports--Records--Juvenile literature.
Classification: DDC 796.32363--dc23

TABLE OF CONTENTS

LUSIA HARRIS

After it began in 1972, the Association of Intercollegiate Athletics for Women (AIAW) Tournament was dominated by several legendary dynasties. For the first three years of the tournament, Immaculata, a small school in Pennsylvania, won the championship. The Mighty Macs returned to the championship game in 1975.

Center Lusia Harris made 63 percent of her shots during her time at Delta State.

This time, they ran straight into Lusia Harris and her undefeated Delta State Lady Statesmen.

A towering 6-foot-3 center, Harris had controlled the paint throughout the 1974–75 season. She was the best player on the court in that season's AIAW title game. The All-American recorded 32 points and 18 rebounds in a 90–81 victory.

The 1975 championship began Delta State's own run of dominance. Harris then led the nation in scoring with 31.2 points per game as a junior in 1975–76. She also led her Mississippi school back to the AIAW championship game. It was a rematch against Immaculata. Once again, the Mighty Macs struggled to slow Harris down. She finished the game with 27 points and 18 rebounds. Delta State secured a second straight title with a 69–64 victory.

In 1976–77, the senior Harris earned All-America honors for the third year in a row. She also helped the Lady Statesmen win their third straight national title. Over the course of the three-peat, Delta State went 93–4, including a perfect 39–0 record at home. Harris finished her career with 2,981 points and 1,662 rebounds, both school records.

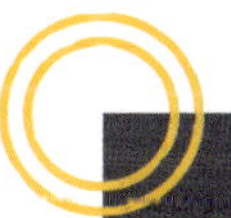

FAST FACT

Harris had a groundbreaking basketball career outside of college. In 1976, she opened scoring in the first-ever Olympic women's basketball game. A year later, the New Orleans Jazz drafted her. Harris is still the only woman to have been selected in the National Basketball Association Draft.

NANCY LIEBERMAN

Nancy Lieberman learned to play basketball on outdoor courts in New York City. She often joined pickup games against boys. The future star quickly developed a knack for physical basketball. In 1976, she brought that toughness to Old Dominion. At 5-foot-10, Lieberman was taller than most point guards. The height allowed her to shoot over smaller defenders. It let her see the whole floor too. Lieberman used her elite vision to set up teammates to score.

As a freshman in 1976–77, Lieberman led Old Dominion to a program-record 23 wins. The Monarchs continued to improve throughout her career. By Lieberman's junior season in 1978–79, she led the Virginia school to its first AIAW Tournament appearance. She then lifted the Monarchs to the semifinals. There, they faced the defending champion University of California, Los Angeles (UCLA) Bruins. Lieberman helped shut down All-America forward Denise Curry and clinch an 87–82 victory.

Next up was the title game against Louisiana Tech. The Lady Techsters came out hot, and the Monarchs were down at halftime.

FAST FACT

Before arriving at Old Dominion, Nancy Lieberman played on the US women's basketball team at the 1976 Olympic Games. She was joined by Lusia Harris and future coaching legend Pat Summitt. The team won a silver medal.

Then Lieberman took control. Her flashy passes kept finding teammates. On defense, the Monarchs played a physical full-court press. Lieberman finished the game with 20 points, and Old Dominion took down Louisiana Tech 75–65.

After the season, Lieberman won the Wade Trophy. That award goes to the best women's player in the country. The next year, she became the first player to win the award twice. Lieberman capped her college career with a 27-game winning streak. In her final game at Old Dominion, she led the Monarchs to a 68–53 victory over Tennessee for a second straight national title.

In 2000, the Nancy Lieberman Award was given out for the first time. That honor goes to the best point guard in the country.

Guard Lynette Woodard earned All-America honors all four years at Kansas.

LYNETTE WOODARD

Lynette Woodard was a star high school player in Wichita, Kansas. After graduating, she decided to stay close to home. Starting in the 1977–78 season, Woodard lifted the Kansas Jayhawks to new heights.

The 5-foot-11 Woodard could play any position on the court. And she showed off her wide range of skills right away. In one January 1978 game, the freshman star set a program record by grabbing 33 rebounds. A month later, she broke Kansas's single-game scoring record when she put up 45 points. Woodard finished her freshman year with 833 points, another school record.

The homegrown star only improved after that. She shattered her own record by scoring 1,117 points as a sophomore. That year, she also set new Jayhawks records for rebounds, blocks, and steals in a season. Her versatile play lifted Kansas to its first Big Eight Conference title.

Woodard went on to help Kansas win the Big Eight again in 1979–80 and 1980–81. During her junior season, she became Kansas's all-time leading scorer. Then, as a senior, she won the Wade Trophy. In her four years at Kansas, Woodard averaged 26.2 points per game. She finished her career with 3,649 points. That stood as the most points in women's college basketball until 2024.

After college, Woodard enjoyed a successful professional and international career. She was the captain of Team USA at the 1984 Olympic Games in Los Angeles. The team won the gold medal. The next year, Woodard became the first female member of the Harlem Globetrotters.

CHERYL MILLER

During her senior year of high school, Cheryl Miller scored 105 points in a single game. Starting in 1981, the 6-foot-3 forward brought her legendary scoring skills to the University of Southern California (USC).

No matter the pressure, the Trojans could count on Miller to sink shots. As a freshman in 1981–82, Miller averaged 20.4 points per game. One year later, she led the Trojans all the way to the 1983 National Collegiate Athletic Association (NCAA) Tournament championship game. Louisiana Tech, winners of the first-ever women's NCAA Tournament in 1982, came into the matchup on a 30-game win streak. But Miller overpowered the Lady Techsters with 27 points, nine rebounds, four blocks, and four steals. Her performance lifted USC to a 69–67 win and its first national title.

Miller continued her tournament heroics in 1984. A title run made USC the first women's team to win back-to-back NCAA championships. The sophomore also earned Final Four Most Outstanding Player (MOP) honors for the second year in a row. She finished the season with an average of 22.0 points and 10.6 rebounds per game. She won the Naismith Trophy, given to the best player in the country.

Miller dominated women's college basketball as a junior and senior too. She led the Trojans back to the national championship game during her senior year. However, they couldn't make it past Texas. Still, Miller's Naismith Trophy win that year made her the first player to win the prestigious honor three times.

Forward Cheryl Miller (31) averaged 23.6 points and 12.0 rebounds per game during her USC career.

Texas center Clarissa Davis (24) won the Naismith Trophy in 1987 and 1989.

CLARISSA DAVIS

In 1982, Texas finished as runners-up in the final AIAW Tournament. For the next three seasons, the Longhorns entered the NCAA Tournament as a No. 2 seed or better. However, each run ended before the Final Four.

Clarissa Davis arrived in Austin, Texas, for the 1985–86 season. The center joined a loaded Longhorns team. And Davis was ready to push them even higher. They entered the 1986 NCAA Tournament with an undefeated record and reached the Final Four at last.

Texas faced Western Kentucky in the semifinals. Davis racked up 32 points and 18 rebounds to spark a blowout 90–65 win. The first-year star was the best player in the championship game as well. Behind 24 points and 14 rebounds from Davis, the Longhorns completed their perfect season. They became the first undefeated NCAA champions.

The 1986 Final Four's MOP only improved as a sophomore. Davis led the Southwest Conference in scoring with 18.6 points per game. After Texas posted a 28–1 record, Davis brought the team back to the Final Four. There, she recorded a double-double of 24 points and 10 rebounds against Louisiana Tech. However, it wasn't enough to take down the Lady Techsters.

Davis missed most of her junior season due to injuries. Back to full health in 1988–89, the senior recorded averages of 26.3 points and 9.9 rebounds per game. Those career-high stats helped her earn her second Naismith Trophy. Davis left Texas with a career scoring average of 19.9 points per game. That set a program record.

JENNIFER AZZI

Jennifer Azzi was a selfless player. The 5-foot-8 point guard always looked for passes that would set up her teammates for scores. Azzi showcased her vision as a freshman at Stanford. In one January 1987 game, Azzi racked up 16 assists. That set a school record for most assists in a game.

Azzi helped out her teammates throughout her college career. In each of her four seasons with the Cardinal, she averaged at least six assists per game. Azzi did more than pass, though. She was also deadly from beyond the arc, making 45 percent of her three-point shots.

Stanford finished 14–14 in 1986–87. The team didn't even make the NCAA Tournament. But the Cardinal improved each year of Azzi's college career. Over the next three seasons, they lost only nine total games. Stanford became a powerhouse in the Pacific-10 (PAC-10) Conference. During her junior year, Azzi won PAC-10 Player of the Year honors while leading the Cardinal to their first conference title.

By 1989–90, Stanford had become one of the country's top teams. That season, the senior Azzi won the Naismith Trophy and helped Stanford cruise to the Final Four. Once there, Azzi showed off her offensive skills. In the semifinal and final, she made 54 percent of her three-pointers. Azzi posted 17 points and five assists in the national championship. Stanford beat Auburn 88–81 to clinch the team's first NCAA title.

Stanford guard Jennifer Azzi earned All-America honors during her junior and senior seasons.

DAWN STALEY

Standing just 5-foot-6, Dawn Staley was often one of the smallest players on the court. The lack of size didn't stop her from taking over games, though. The point guard transformed Virginia when she arrived in 1988–89.

Staley was a stellar two-way player. She could both attack the rim and bury long jump shots. She also had great passing skills.

In 15 NCAA Tournament games, Virginia guard Dawn Staley averaged 18.3 points per game.

However, Staley's biggest strength was her defense. Opponents struggled to dribble past the physical guard. And Staley's tireless motor allowed her to rack up steals.

As a sophomore, Staley went on a postseason tear. She averaged 27.0 points and 4.3 steals per game in the first three rounds of the 1990 NCAA Tournament. That lifted Virginia to its first Final Four appearance. However, Staley's 18 points weren't enough for the Cavaliers to defeat Stanford.

In 1990–91, Staley led the Atlantic Coast Conference (ACC) in steals and assists per game. The all-around play earned her the Naismith Trophy. Staley also led Virginia on another run to the Final Four. This time, the Cavaliers defeated the University of Connecticut (UConn) and moved on to the championship game. There, Virginia faced Tennessee. Staley put on a show. She recorded 28 points, 11 rebounds, six assists, and three steals. However, Tennessee prevailed in overtime.

Virginia's star point guard remained consistent throughout her career. As a senior, she posted nearly identical stats to her impressive junior year. Staley helped the Cavaliers reach the Final Four for the third straight year. They lost to Stanford, but Staley's amazing performance that season earned her a second Naismith Trophy.

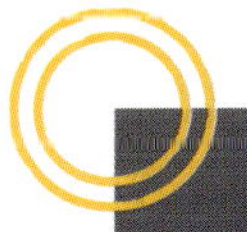

FAST FACT

Virginia lost the 1991 women's national championship game. But Staley was still named Final Four MOP. She became the only player from a losing team to win the award.

SHERYL SWOOPES

Sheryl Swoopes originally planned to play basketball at nearby University of Texas in her native state. However, the 6-foot forward transferred from there to a junior college called South Plains College before ever playing with the Longhorns. She spent the next two years dominating the opposition. Swoopes earned All-America honors both seasons. In 1990–91, she was the National Junior College Player of the Year.

Before her junior year, Swoopes transferred again. This time, she went to Texas Tech. Stronger competition in the Southwest Conference didn't slow Swoopes down. During her first season with the Lady Raiders, she led the conference in scoring. She also led Texas Tech to its first regular-season conference title. The Lady Raiders then went on to win the conference championship as well.

Swoopes helped Texas Tech defend both of those titles in 1992–93. Meanwhile, she led the nation in scoring. Once the NCAA Tournament started, Swoopes elevated her game even more. Through the first four rounds, she scored at least 30 points per game. She grabbed at least 10 rebounds as well. Her four double-doubles led Texas Tech to the national championship game.

In the title game, Ohio State couldn't do anything to stop Swoopes. By the end of the game, she had taken six three-pointers. She made all of them. And she sank all 11 of her free throw attempts. Swoopes finished the game with a championship-record 47 points. The historic performance lifted Texas Tech to an 84–82 win.

Forward Sheryl Swoopes celebrates Texas Tech's 1993 national championship victory.

CHAMIQUE HOLDSCLAW

Tennessee boasted a talented roster in 1995–96. Even so, freshman Chamique Holdsclaw quickly proved she was the team's best player. The 6-foot-2 forward led the Lady Volunteers in scoring that year.

It wasn't all easy, though. Two weeks before the 1996 NCAA Tournament, Holdsclaw injured her knee. She decided to play through

Starting in 1996–97, Tennessee forward Chamique Holdsclaw led her conference in scoring for three straight seasons.

the pain. The tough freshman lifted Tennessee to the Final Four. There, the Lady Vols defeated UConn in overtime. Next was the national championship. Facing Southeastern Conference (SEC) foe Georgia, Holdsclaw took over. The All-American overcame her injury and posted 16 points and 14 rebounds. She powered the Lady Vols to an 83–65 victory and a national title.

Holdsclaw was just getting started. In the 1997 NCAA Tournament, the sophomore led the Lady Vols in scoring in each of their six games. After lifting Tennessee to another title, Holdsclaw earned the Final Four MOP.

Holdsclaw improved even more as a junior. She led the highest scoring offense in the country for the 1997–98 season. Holdsclaw then averaged 26.3 points per game in the NCAA Tournament. That helped the Lady Vols close out an undefeated season and secure the first three-peat in NCAA women's basketball history. Holdsclaw also won the Naismith Trophy.

Holdsclaw didn't finish her career with a fourth national championship. Tennessee was upset in the Elite Eight in 1999. After showing her talent all year, though, Holdsclaw won the Naismith Trophy for the second straight year.

FAST FACT

Holdsclaw played at her best in the NCAA Tournament. She scored 479 points over 22 games. She also grabbed 198 rebounds. Both totals set tournament records.

RUTH RILEY

Whenever Ruth Riley got close to the basket, Notre Dame opponents were in trouble. The 6-foot-5 center was a menace in the paint. She dominated on both offense and defense.

In 1998–99, Riley posted a conference-high 3.3 blocks per game. The sophomore also boasted the conference's best field-goal percentage. She went on to match those feats as a junior and senior. Her shot-blocking ability helped her win Big East Defensive Player of the Year honors three times.

Riley achieved all of this under the shadow of a giant in the conference. By the late 1990s, UConn had established itself as the power of the Big East. Riley wasn't fazed. During her senior year in 2000–01, she helped Notre Dame earn a share of the Big East regular-season title. The Fighting Irish had never done that before. Then she helped her team reach new heights in the 2001 NCAA Tournament.

The No. 1 seed Fighting Irish made a run to the Final Four. With fellow No. 1 seed UConn standing in their way, Riley blocked five shots in a 90–75 win. The star center played even better in the championship game against Purdue. Riley blocked seven shots and grabbed 13 rebounds.

Notre Dame was trailing 66–64 with just over a minute to go. Riley buried a shot to tie the game. On Notre Dame's next offensive possession, Purdue fouled Riley with 5.8 seconds left. She calmly sank two free throws to take the lead. Her 28 points lifted the Fighting Irish to their first national title.

Notre Dame center Ruth Riley won the Naismith Trophy as a senior in 2001.

DIANA TAURASI

UConn was already a national powerhouse when Diana Taurasi joined the team in 2000–01. Adding the sharpshooter only made the Huskies better. UConn lost to Notre Dame in the Final Four in

UConn guard Diana Taurasi (3) won the Naismith Trophy as a junior and again as a senior.

Taurasi's freshman year. Over the next three years, the 6-foot guard didn't experience another loss in the NCAA Tournament.

In 2001–02, UConn entered the NCAA Tournament undefeated. Taurasi provided consistent scoring. The Huskies won each of their six games by at least 12 points. They capped off the perfect season with an 82–70 win over Oklahoma.

By her junior year, Taurasi had established herself as UConn's leader. She often took the biggest shots in a game. The competitive, trash-talking guard finished the year as the team's top scorer and rebounder.

However, Taurasi's real heroics came in the 2003 NCAA Tournament. She saved UConn multiple times. With 12 minutes left in the Final Four, the Huskies trailed Texas by nine points. Then Taurasi took control. She started hitting shots from long range and drawing fouls at the rim. Taurasi finished the game with 26 points, and the Huskies managed a comeback victory. After the win, legendary UConn coach Geno Auriemma explained how his team won. "We have Diana Taurasi, and they don't," he said. Next up was a matchup against Tennessee. Taurasi scored 28 as the Huskies won 73–68. That made UConn the first team to win a national title without a senior on its roster.

As a senior, Taurasi led the Huskies back to the national championship game. Once again, they faced Tennessee. In a battle between the sport's two dominant programs, Taurasi scored 17 points in a 70–61 win. UConn secured a three-peat of its own.

SEIMONE AUGUSTUS

Seimone Augustus adjusted to college competition right away. In her first game at Louisiana State University (LSU), the 6-foot-1 guard scored a team-high 27 points. Over the next four years, she piled up many more high-scoring games.

A native of Baton Rouge, Louisiana, Augustus grew up playing in local pickup games. The skills she learned there helped her transform her hometown college into a national power. In 2003, the first-year star helped LSU earn its first-ever No. 1 seed in the NCAA Tournament. The Tigers then made it to the Elite Eight.

As a sophomore, Augustus scored a career-high 29 points in the Sweet 16 against Texas. She matched that total in the Elite Eight against Georgia. However, the Tigers' run ended in the Final Four when they lost a 52–50 nail-biter against Tennessee.

LSU had never won an SEC regular-season title before. Over the next two years, Augustus led the Tigers to two. During that span, they lost only one conference game. Augustus also won the Naismith Trophy as a junior and as a senior.

Augustus couldn't quite break through in the NCAA Tournament, however. In 2005, she led the Tigers back to the Final Four, but they lost to the eventual champion Baylor Bears. The next season, Augustus had a clutch game against Stanford in the Elite Eight. Late in the second half, she drew a charge to maintain LSU's one-point lead. She then hit two free throws to send LSU to its third straight Final Four. Once again, the Tigers fell short. But Augustus had made her mark on the college game.

LSU guard Seimone Augustus (33) won SEC Player of the Year as a junior and senior.

CANDACE PARKER

Candace Parker first dunked a basketball when she was 15 years old. She continued to throw down slams throughout high school. The forward joined Tennessee before the 2004–05 season. But she couldn't play due to a knee injury.

After recovering, Parker quickly proved that the injury hadn't taken away her athleticism. Tennessee faced Army in her NCAA

Tennessee center Candace Parker led the SEC in scoring during her sophomore and junior seasons.

Tournament debut. The sophomore star ran down the court on a fast break. She finished the play with an emphatic slam dunk. That made Parker the first woman to dunk in an NCAA Tournament game. She had the tournament's second dunk too, after slamming it down again in the second half.

Parker did much more than just dunk. On offense, she could score in the post with midrange jumpers. On defense, she could shut down almost any opponent. Parker used her 6-foot-4 frame to constantly swat down shots. During her three years at Tennessee, she averaged 2.5 blocks per game.

In the 2007 NCAA Tournament, Parker anchored a tough Tennessee defense. The Lady Vols allowed an average of only 49.1 points per game. They gave up even fewer in the championship game, dominating Rutgers in a 59–46 rout.

Parker looked poised to lead Tennessee on another deep tournament run. Things looked bleak after she dislocated her left shoulder during the Elite Eight. However, Parker played through the pain and led the Lady Vols back into the Final Four. There, the still-injured Parker had 15 rebounds in the semifinal. Then, the 2008 Naismith Trophy winner scored 17 points in the final to help Tennessee successfully defend its championship. The senior ended her career on top.

FAST FACT

Parker competed in a dunk contest while she was in high school. She went up against the top boys' players in the country. Her one-handed slams helped her take first place.

TINA CHARLES

Tina Charles thrived in the post. The 6-foot-4 UConn center punished smaller defenders close to the basket. As a freshman in 2006–07, she made 59 percent of her shots. For the rest of her college career, she drained more than 60 percent of her attempts. Charles also used her height to grab plenty of rebounds. She finished her career with a UConn-record 1,367 total boards.

Charles's dominant post presence, paired with star guard Maya Moore, helped UConn stack up wins. After losing in the Final Four as a sophomore, Charles wouldn't be denied in the 2009 NCAA Tournament. She recorded three double-doubles to help UConn return to the Final Four. Then UConn moved on to the national championship with an 83–64 victory over Stanford.

The Huskies faced Louisville in the title game. Charles made 11 of her 13 shots and scored 25 points. She also grabbed 19 rebounds. When it was all over, UConn had closed out an undefeated season. Charles added a second trophy as the Final Four's MOP.

Charles continued to rack up points and rebounds as a senior. Her efficient scoring helped her win the Naismith Trophy. Meanwhile, UConn continued to roll over the competition. The Huskies entered the 2010 NCAA Tournament on a 72-game winning streak. That continued to the final as Charles averaged 10.3 rebounds per game in the postseason. Facing Stanford for the national title, Charles showcased her defensive skills and blocked six shots. The Huskies won 53–47. That made UConn the first team to complete two straight perfect seasons.

Center Tina Charles (31) earned All-America honors three times.

MAYA MOORE

There was almost nothing Maya Moore couldn't do on a basketball court. The 6-foot forward could make crafty drives to the basket. She could also drain three-pointers. If she was getting too much attention from defenses, Moore would find teammates for open shots. Those skills helped her become a first-team All-American as a freshman in 2007–08. She went on to earn that honor in all four of her seasons with UConn.

Guard Maya Moore won Big East Player of the Year honors three times at UConn.

Moore wasn't just an offensive star. She was willing to do whatever it took to win. Her size and quickness allowed her to guard multiple positions. And her relentless drive helped her snag rebounds.

When Moore shared the court with center Tina Charles, UConn was nearly unstoppable. The Huskies lost only two games during Moore's and Charles's freshman year. Nobody beat UConn during their sophomore season. Moore won her first Naismith Trophy that year.

The duo led UConn into the 2010 NCAA Tournament undefeated too. Then Moore went on a tear. She recorded 34 points and 12 rebounds to beat Baylor in the Final Four. Next up was the title game against Stanford. UConn started slow. At halftime, the Huskies trailed 20–12. But Moore went off in the second half. She finished the game with 23 points and 11 rebounds as UConn finished another perfect season.

The Huskies went on to win an NCAA-record 90 games straight. Their streak finally ended with a loss to Stanford in December 2010. Moore hardly slowed down. She also led UConn back to the Final Four. But even her 36 points weren't enough to lift UConn past Notre Dame. Despite the loss, Moore still wrapped up her senior year with a second Naismith Trophy.

FAST FACT

UConn has featured many legendary women's players. But none of those legends scored as much as Moore. She finished her career with a program-record 3,036 points.

BRITTNEY GRINER

Brittney Griner arrived at Baylor for the 2009–10 season. The 6-foot-8 center was one of the tallest players in the history of women's college basketball. And she knew how to make the most of her height advantage.

Griner blocked 223 shots as a freshman. That shattered the previous NCAA record. Griner showed off her defensive dominance in the 2010 NCAA Tournament. Facing Georgetown in the second round, she blocked 14 shots. That set a record for most blocks in an NCAA Tournament game. The Bears went all the way to the Final Four, where they fell to UConn.

Griner also used her height on offense. She became deadly in the post. Starting in 2010–11, Griner led the Big 12 Conference in scoring for three years straight. Her elite offense wasn't enough for a title run in 2011, though. Baylor lost in the Elite Eight.

Griner was more motivated than ever in 2011–12. The junior star put together all her skills. That season, she averaged 23.2 points, 9.5 rebounds, and 5.2 blocks per game and earned the Naismith Trophy. The Bears rolled into the national championship game with

FAST FACT

Griner blocked at least 149 shots every season at Baylor. She finished her career with an NCAA record 748 blocks. That was 80 more blocks than any other player in NCAA history.

an undefeated record. Facing Notre Dame, Griner had another legendary performance. She recorded 26 points, 13 rebounds, and five blocks as Baylor won its first-ever title.

As a senior, Griner led the Bears to a 32-game win streak. However, Baylor lost steam in the 2013 NCAA Tournament, losing in the Sweet 16. Still, Griner's dominant play was enough to earn her a second Naismith Trophy.

Center Brittney Griner averaged 5.1 blocks per game with Baylor.

BREANNA STEWART

UConn freshman Breanna Stewart couldn't seem to beat Notre Dame in 2012–13. The Huskies lost by one point in a January 2013 home game during her freshman year. In a rematch at Notre Dame a few months later, UConn fell short in triple overtime. Then, in the Big East Tournament, the Fighting Irish won by two.

Forward Breanna Stewart made 53 percent of her shots at UConn.

The fourth meeting came in the 2013 Final Four. This time, Stewart was ready. The 6-foot-4 forward scored a career-high 29 points to help UConn take down their rival 83–65. Stewart stepped up again in the national championship game. Her 23 points and nine rebounds lifted UConn to a blowout win over Louisville. Stewart became the first freshman since 1987 to win Final Four MOP.

Stewart's 2013 tournament run sparked one of the greatest careers in college basketball history. As a sophomore, she led UConn in points and blocks per game. Her two-way play helped UConn finish the season a perfect 40–0. After rolling through the 2014 NCAA Tournament, Stewart locked down a second title.

In the second game of her junior season, Stewart played 44 of a possible 45 minutes in an overtime game against Stanford. Despite 23 points and 10 rebounds from the star forward, UConn lost by two. Stewart went on to play 75 more games at UConn after that. She won them all. Those wins, including two more championships, added to the most dominant career women's college basketball had ever seen.

FAST FACT

Stewart won her third consecutive Naismith Trophy as a senior in 2015–16. She joined Cheryl Miller as the only women's players to win the award three times. Stewart also became the only player to earn Final Four MOP four times. No other player had won that more than twice.

A'JA WILSON

The South Carolina Gamecocks had never been to a Final Four before A'ja Wilson arrived in 2014–15. In fact, they had not even won an SEC Tournament. Wilson helped South Carolina achieve both those feats in her first year.

As a freshman, the 6-foot-5 forward provided reliable offense off the bench for the Gamecocks. In the program's first-ever Final Four game, she recorded 20 points and nine rebounds. She added four blocks as well. But South Carolina fell 66–65 to Notre Dame.

Wilson became a regular starter as a sophomore. She was a skilled two-way player. On offense, she could create her own shots with ease. On defense, she could deny opponents at the rim or on the perimeter.

The three-time SEC Player of the Year continued to lift her team to success. As a junior in 2016–17, Wilson led South Carolina back to the Final Four. In the semifinals matchup against Stanford, Wilson racked up 13 points and 19 rebounds. South Carolina won 62–53. Next, she put up an all-time performance in the championship game. She scored 23 points and grabbed 10 rebounds. On defense, she added four blocks. Her all-around play clinched the Gamecocks' first national title.

Wilson carried the momentum into her senior season. She posted career highs in points, rebounds, and blocks per game in 2017–18. South Carolina fell short of a second title, but Wilson's improvements won her a Naismith Trophy.

South Carolina forward A'ja Wilson averaged 11.8 rebounds per game in 2017–18.

CAITLIN CLARK

Caitlin Clark wasted no time becoming one of the best players in college basketball. The 6-foot guard scored 26.6 points per game as a freshman at Iowa. That made her the nation's leading scorer for the 2020–21 season.

Clark often drained shots from well beyond the three-point line. But she could also dribble past defenders to score in the paint. On top

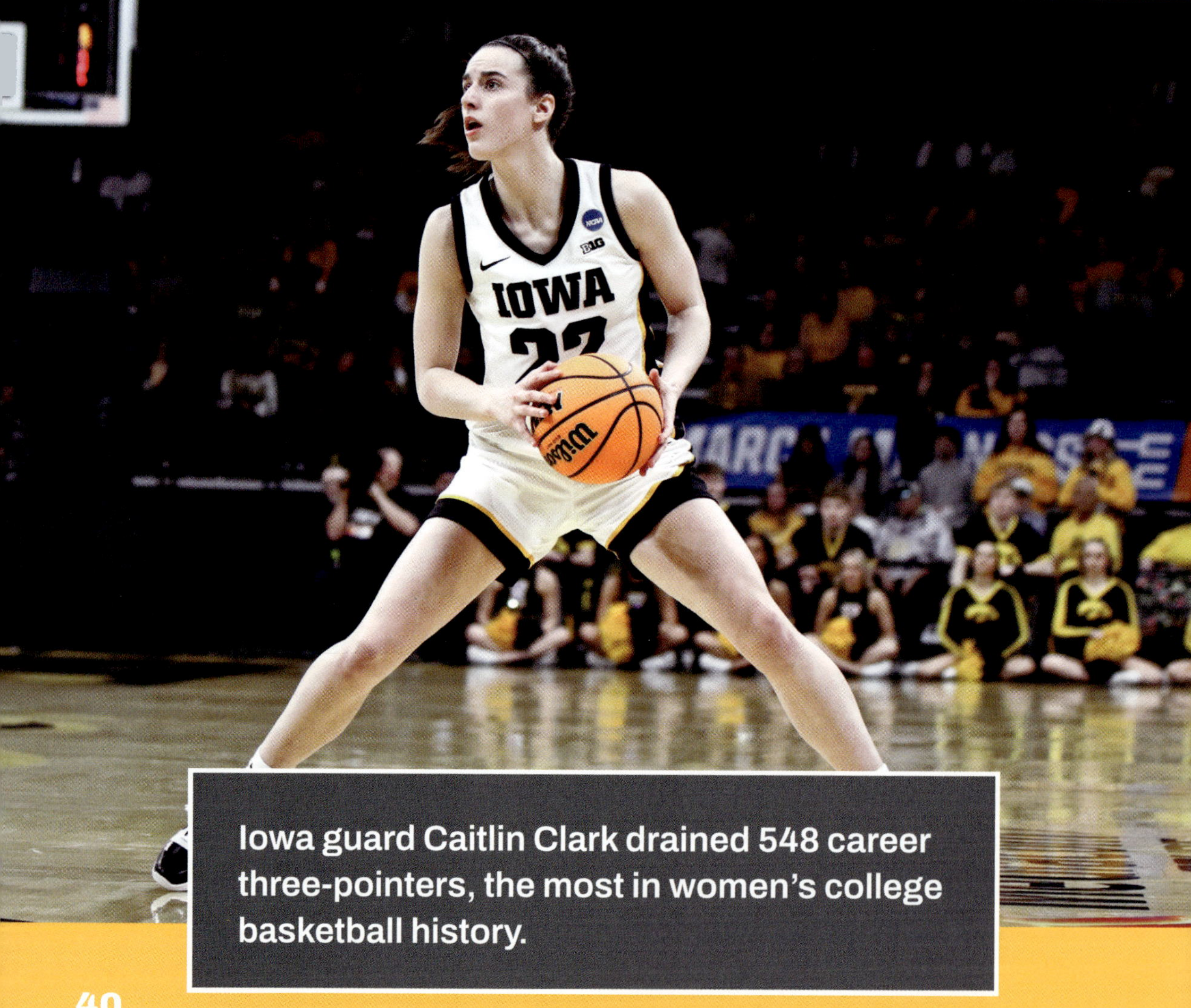

Iowa guard Caitlin Clark drained 548 career three-pointers, the most in women's college basketball history.

of her scoring, she had elite vision. Starting in her sophomore year, Clark led the nation in assists per game for three straight seasons.

A native of West Des Moines, Iowa, Clark had always dreamed of taking her home state's Hawkeyes to the Final Four. In the 2023 NCAA Tournament, Iowa rolled to the Elite Eight. Clark then recorded a triple-double of 41 points, 10 rebounds, and 12 assists. The Hawkeyes beat Louisville 97–83 and moved on to their first Final Four in 30 years. The No. 2 seed Iowa faced an undefeated South Carolina team. Behind another 41-point performance from Clark, the Hawkeyes upset the No. 1 Gamecocks. Clark then buried eight three-pointers in the championship game. However, it wasn't enough to beat LSU.

Clark scored 1,234 points as a senior. That shattered the NCAA women's single-season scoring record. She also won a second straight Naismith Trophy. In the 2024 Elite Eight, she got a chance for revenge against LSU. Clark scorched the Tigers with 41 points and 12 assists. This time, the Hawkeyes came out on top. Iowa then beat UConn in the Final Four and moved to the championship. Clark had a hot start in her last college game. She scored 18 points in the first quarter against South Carolina. However, it wasn't enough to take down the powerhouse Gamecocks.

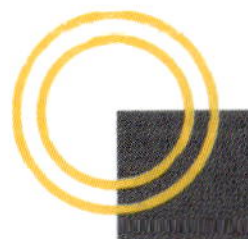

FAST FACT

During her senior season, Clark passed Lynette Woodard as the leading scorer in women's college basketball history. About a week later, she bested Pete Maravich for the most points in both men's and women's college basketball. Clark finished her career with 3,951 points.

PAIGE BUECKERS

In 2020, Paige Bueckers was named the best high school girls' basketball player in the country. A year later, she was the best player in college basketball. She became the first women's freshman to win the Naismith Trophy. Leading her team in points and assists per game, the rising star lifted the Huskies to the Final Four.

A 6-foot guard, Bueckers almost always made the right play on offense. She often looked to set up her teammates for easy buckets. She drained jumpers from all over the court too. The efficient scorer made 53 percent of her shots, including 43 percent of her three-point attempts.

An injury forced Bueckers to miss more than half of her sophomore season. She returned in time for the 2022 NCAA Tournament, though. In the Elite Eight, UConn faced North Carolina State. Bueckers scored 27 points as the Huskies won in double overtime. UConn then took down Stanford 63–58 in the Final Four. But the Huskies couldn't lock down a win against South Carolina in the championship game.

Another injury sidelined Bueckers for the entire 2022–23 season. Returning to health in 2023–24, she posted a career-high 21.9 points per game. She then lifted the Huskies back to the Final Four. But Iowa ended their run there.

With one last chance to win a title in 2024–25, Bueckers couldn't be denied. In the Sweet 16, she scored a career-high 40 points against Oklahoma. That made her the first UConn player to score 40 points in a tournament game. Bueckers then recorded 31 points and six assists in the Elite Eight. The Huskies went on to win both their semifinal and final games by more than 20 points. With Bueckers leading the way, UConn won its first national title in nine years.

Guard Paige Bueckers averaged a school-record 19.8 points per game during her UConn career.

HONORABLE MENTIONS

ANN MEYERS

Meyers was the first player to make four All-America teams. As a senior in 1978, the UCLA guard led her team to the AIAW national title.

ANNE DONOVAN

A 6-foot-8 center, Donovan helped Old Dominion win the 1980 AIAW title. As a senior in 1982–83, she won the inaugural women's Naismith Trophy.

REBECCA LOBO

In 1994–95, Lobo led an undefeated UConn team to its first national title. The senior center also won the Naismith Trophy.

TAMIKA CATCHINGS

A four-time All-American at Tennessee, Catchings helped the Lady Volunteers go undefeated in 1997–98. The forward also won the Naismith Trophy in 1999–2000.

SUE BIRD

Bird ran UConn's offense as a pass-first point guard and helped the Huskies win titles in 2000 and 2002. She also won the Naismith Trophy in 2001–02.

KELSEY PLUM

As a junior in 2016, Plum lifted Washington to its first Final Four. The point guard then averaged 31.7 points per game as a senior and finished her career as the leading scorer in NCAA women's basketball.

SABRINA IONESCU

Ionescu did a little bit of everything for Oregon. The sharpshooting guard lifted the Ducks to their first Final Four in 2019. She had a record 26 career triple-doubles.

ALIYAH BOSTON

Boston played in three Final Fours with South Carolina. The forward received the Naismith Trophy and won a national title in 2021–22.

GLOSSARY

conference
A group of schools that join together to create a league for their sports teams.

debut
First appearance.

double-double
Accumulating 10 or more of two certain statistics in a game.

efficient
Performing well without many mistakes.

fast break
Moving the ball up the floor quickly.

junior college
A two-year college that often includes athletic programs.

midrange
The area of the court inside the three-point line and outside of the paint.

post
The area around the basket where power forwards and centers usually play.

triple-double
Accumulating 10 or more of three certain statistics in a game.

two-way player
Someone who plays both offense and defense well.

upset
An unexpected victory by a supposedly weaker team or player.

versatile
Able to perform many different roles or functions.

vision
The ability to see how a play is developing and to know what will happen next.

MORE INFORMATION

BOOKS

Big Book of Who Women in Sports: The 101 Stars Every Fan Needs to Know. Triumph, 2025.

Giedd, Steph. *Basketball Strategies*. Abdo, 2024.

Hanlon, Luke. *Everything Basketball*. Abdo, 2024.

ONLINE RESOURCES

To learn more about the GOATs of college women's basketball, please visit **abdobooklinks.com** or scan this QR code. These links are routinely monitored and updated to provide the most current information available.

INDEX

ABOUT THE AUTHOR

Luke Hanlon is a sportswriter and editor based in Minneapolis, Minnesota. He's written dozens of nonfiction sports books for young people and spends a lot of his free time watching his favorite Minnesota sports teams.